BEAT PANIC

BULLET GUIDE

Hodder Education, 338 Euston Road, London NW1 3BH

Hodder Education is an Hachette UK company

First published in UK 2012 by Hodder Education

This edition published 2012

www.hoddereducation.co.uk

Typeset by Stephen Rowling/Springworks

Printed in Spain

BEAT PANIC

BULLET GUIDE

Martha Langley

Acknowledgements

Thanks to everyone who helped with quotes and case histories.

The sub-personalities mentioned in Chapter 9 were first described by Dr R. Reid Wilson.

About the author

Martha Langley is the author of *Mindfulness Made Easy* and co-author of *Free Yourself from Anxiety*. She spent more than 15 years as a volunteer on various mental health helplines, and was also a mentor for people working to recover from anxiety disorders.

Contents

Introduction

Panic attacks are far more common than is generally supposed. Many sufferers try to hide their panic, either out of embarrassment or from thinking they're to blame in some way. All of us, probably unwittingly, know at least one person who suffers from repeated panic attacks, and yet many people still feel that it's a rare, or even unique, problem.

It can take a while even to realize that panic is the problem. It is important to have your physical health checked, of course, but eventually you may have to accept that your own mind is causing these terrifying experiences.

Panic can seem so overwhelming that it's easy to feel that the cure must have to be something pretty drastic – or perhaps that there is no cure. This is not the case, and there is a lot of help available.

Doctors and therapists have realized over the years that there is a lot that people can do themselves to help deal with panic. A lot of the advice is pretty basic – eat well, get enough sleep, manage your stress – and yet it's surprising how many people neglect their own most basic needs.

This simple approach, together with learning to face your fear, will be helpful to many people. Others will need to seek out professional help in addition, but no one needs to suffer in silence. The therapy of choice at the moment is cognitive–behavioural therapy. As the name suggests, the aim is to help you to change both your behaviour and your thinking (or cognition).

Just remember, panic can be beaten.

1 Panic explained

Fight or flight drives panic

A primitive survival mechanism that gives you the energy to run away or stay and fight

• •

The earliest people were surrounded by threats and faced a constant battle for survival. They could either **run away** from danger or face it and **fight back**. Whichever they chose took **energy**, so the **fight-or-flight** mechanism evolved.

It releases chemicals such as adrenaline to provide a rush of physical energy. The same thing happens when you have a panic attack. You feel threatened, and the fight-or-flight mechanism kicks into action.

- When you're frightened you get ready for **action**.
- When the fear passes, you can **relax**.
- A panic attack is a massive and **irrational** fear response.
- It starts with a thought, then your nervous system takes charge.
- **Fear** of having another panic attack can impact on your life.

Panic is like a fear of the unknown, like everything is closing in on me.

Mal

Fight or flight

When something happens to frighten you, your brain prepares your body for **action**:

* Your heart beats faster.
* Your breathing gets faster and deeper.

In an instant you are all pumped up and ready to go.

Once you've had the initial thought, 'I'm scared', everything else happens automatically. Your involuntary nervous system takes over and makes sure that you're **ready for action** – no time for analysis and deep thought – you have to think on your feet and make instant decisions.

The physical sensations are very unpleasant but, if you're really scared, you'll hardly notice them.

Once the danger has passed your brain instructs your nervous system to **turn off** the fight-or-flight mechanism.

* Your heart slows down.
* Your breathing slows down.

You may feel a little shaky, but you quickly return to normal.

Your body needs time to recover from the fright, and time to replenish the resources that were put into that great surge of energy. You need to **relax** for a while.

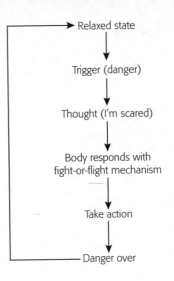

Relaxed state

↓

Trigger (danger)

↓

Thought (I'm scared)

↓

Body responds with fight-or-flight mechanism

↓

Take action

↓

Danger over

5

Panic

When you have a panic attack, something **triggers** your fight-or-flight mechanism, but you probably won't know what it is. You'll just know that you feel terrified. You can feel any of these symptoms (but probably not all of them):

* can't breathe
* choking
* heart racing
* tight chest
* tight muscles
* trembling

* numb
* sweaty
* dizzy
* sick
* needing the toilet.

Fight or flight is designed to be **short lived**, so a panic attack doesn't usually last very long, although at the time it can seem like forever.

Panic attacks appear to come out of the blue. One minute you're fine, and the next you're gasping for breath, your heart racing, and so on.

Most people react with flight – they might:

* **leave** the meeting or class
* **run out** of the restaurant or shop
* **get off** the bus or train.

Usually you start to feel better quite quickly. As you calm down, your mind starts to search for an explanation. Most people ask one of two questions:

1 Am I going mad?
2 Have I got something wrong with my heart?

The answer to both is usually 'No', but always get your health checked to be sure.

Your nervous system

The fight-or-flight response is controlled by your **involuntary**, or autonomic, **nervous system**. This part of your nervous system runs your body without you having to consciously think about it: your heartbeat, your digestion, and so on.

When you think about a conscious action, such as picking up this book, there's always a slight delay as your brain sends the signal to your **voluntary**, or somatic, **nervous system**. At times of danger, speed is of the essence, and so fight or flight is an **instant reaction** that you don't have to think about or decide to do.

This is why panic attacks happen so quickly and seem to be **out of** your **control**.

Even so, the fight-or-flight response always starts with a **thought**, and so does panic. The thought usually happens so quickly that you're not aware of it. Typical thoughts are:

* I can't stand this.
* I'm going to pass out.
* I'm going to be sick.
* I'll die of embarrassment if anyone notices.
* I can't cope.
* I can't face another panic attack.

Once you've had the thought, your involuntary nervous system takes over and creates the fight-or-flight response. Once the panic attack has started, it can feel as if there's nothing you can do to stop it, and it feels unbearable.

Getting help

Your first panic attack can be so frightening that you live in **terror** of having another one. You may **avoid** the place where it happened, then start avoiding other places. Some people end up **housebound**.

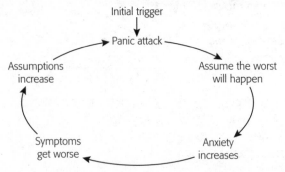

Initial trigger
→ Panic attack
Assume the worst will happen
Anxiety increases
Symptoms get worse
Assumptions increase

There is a lot you can do to help yourself. Your doctor can refer you for cognitive–behavioural therapy, or counselling. While you're waiting for your appointment, try to **help yourself** – it can be done.

10

Self-help has three aspects:

* reducing your **background anxiety** by taking care of yourself
* looking at the **source** of your anxiety by examining stress factors
* learning to **cope with panic** through breathing exercises and dealing with negative thoughts.

This all takes **time**, so be prepared to rearrange your schedule.

It also takes **commitment**, so be prepared to stick at it.

2 Relax

Training yourself in relaxation

Regular relaxation is a key skill for dealing with panic

Relaxation exercises are a **simple** and **effective** way of countering panic. They need to be done once or twice a day for several weeks. Use a CD or an audio download, so that you can lie back and let the voice guide you.

This is not the same as relaxing in front of the TV, or stopping for a coffee. It is **full, deep physical and mental relaxation**.

* Relaxation is **essential** when dealing with panic.
* Do a relaxation exercise **every day** using an audio recording.
* You can use muscle relaxation or visualization.
* Set aside at least half an hour for relaxation.
* If you're anxious about letting go, take it **gently**.
* Increase the time you spend on soothing activities.
* You can create your own recording.

Panic attacks feed on themselves, so find a way to break the cycle.
Ann

Relaxation exercises

There are two main types of relaxation exercise:

1 progressive **muscle** relaxation, in which you clench and relax muscles in turn
2 **visualization**, in which you imagine being in a peaceful place such as a garden or a beach.

Use whichever type appeals to you most, and try several recordings, until you find the one that works best for you. The important thing is to play it **every single day**, at least once and preferably twice. It will take 30–40 minutes.

You always have a choice. One way is to learn basic strategies to lower the physical intensity of panic.

Mo

16

What you need for relaxation:

* somewhere **private** to lie down or sit back
* a **comfortable** bed or chair
* no interruptions
* the telephone turned off.

The best times of day to do relaxation exercises are early morning and early evening. Look at your schedule to see if you can manage this, but any time is better than not doing it at all.

If you think you're too busy to do relaxation, then remind yourself how much you hate it when panic strikes. Find the time.

TOP TIP
If you worry about falling asleep and sleeping for too long, then set a timer.

Dealing with difficulties

Give yourself time to get used to the feeling of being fully relaxed

Some people feel anxious about relaxing – it feels like letting go.
Try these tips:

* Listen to the recording first without lying back. That way you'll learn to **trust** the voice.
* Start by playing it through to the end **every day**, even if you can't relax.
* Don't judge yourself. There's no exam to pass, and **no right or wrong** way.
* Play it every day for three weeks to give it a fair chance.
* If you fall into a deep sleep, that's OK. You must have been tired.

If you do only one thing to beat panic, then relaxation is the one to choose. The more you listen to the recording, the more your **background anxiety** will go down.

While you're relaxing, your mind and body can **replace the resources** that are used up during panic.

You can use the recording to help you **sleep** at night, but don't count that as one of your regular sessions.

TOP TIP
Choose your **favourite phrase** from the recording and repeat it to yourself at times of stress. If you've been doing regular relaxation, the phrase will remind you of the feeling, and you'll be able to relax.

Making it work

* Before you start your relaxation session, it can be helpful to do gentle **stretches** for a few minutes.
* Tell yourself that while you're listening to the recording, you'll let go of all your daily concerns. Most things can wait half an hour.
* Imagine yourself feeling **warm** and **heavy**, and let these feelings increase as the time goes by.
* If any anxious thoughts come into your mind, let them **float** away – think of them as balloons drifting away from you.

Once you have regular relaxation exercises in place, you can look at other ways of winding down. Don't choose anything that makes you panicky – seek out activities that are **peaceful** and **calming**, such as:

* listening to music
* having a bath
* reading a book or magazine
* yoga

* pursuing a hobby that absorbs you – craft work, gardening or anything else creative is particularly good.

Full relaxation combined with these other activities will increase your **relaxation response** and reduce your anxiety levels.

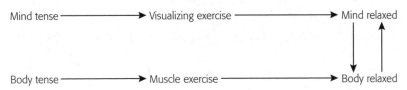

Creating your own version

You can record your own voice, rather than talking, if you find that more **soothing**.

For progressive **muscle** relaxation, make a list before you start. Speak **slowly**, leaving long pauses between each set of muscles:

* Start by clenching your toes and then relaxing them.
* Repeat with your feet, then your calves.
* Mention each muscle in turn, working up your legs and body to your head.
* Lift your shoulders, then release them.
* Work down your arms to your hands.
* Don't forget your face and forehead – screw up your eyes, then open your mouth wide.
* For the back of your neck, press your head back to tighten the muscles.

You can record your own **visualization**. Write it out first and speak slowly and softly.

Choose a place that you find **peaceful** – somewhere outdoors is best. It can be a real place or an imagined one. Good examples are:

* a garden
* a beach
* a forest

* the top of a hill in the countryside
* a riverside.

Remember to:

* Describe the place in detail.
* Dwell on the **beauty** and **peace** that you find there.
* Imagine you are alone there, quietly enjoying your own company.
* Fill the picture with natural sights and sounds.
* Choose weather that pleases you.

3 Get active

Exercise beats panic

If you don't already have an exercise routine, now's the time to start

• •

Exercise that gets you out of breath – aerobic exercise – has multiple benefits for anyone trying to deal with panic.

When exercise makes you breathe hard, your breathing returns to **normal** afterwards. When your muscles are working hard, you **let go** of the tensions that arise from stress.

Exercise encourages your brain to produce **mood-enhancing** chemicals. At the end of a session, you'll be physically **relaxed**.

- Exercise helps with your **breathing**, your **muscle tension** and your **mood.**
- Check with your doctor, and build up your fitness **gradually**.
- Choose an activity that gets you out of breath.
- Exercise three times a week for 30 minutes.
- Exercise increases serotonin and endorphin levels.
- Rhythmic exercise is **soothing**.

... good exercise, keeping as fit as possible ...
Mal

Exercise options

Most people can find a way to exercise – you don't have to **run** a marathon or **swim** the Channel. If you haven't exercised for a while or you have a health problem, then check with your doctor before you start.

It's OK to start **small**. You can start at home, with an exercise DVD or a video games console. If you feel really unfit, start with the **warm-up** and see how that goes.

28

If you enjoy **sport**, then you've a lot of choices for your exercise regime, but don't despair if you're not the competitive type. As long as the exercise is **vigorous** enough to get you out of breath it will do the trick. You can:

* walk briskly .
* jog
* go to the gym
* dance

* swim
* dig the garden
* vacuum the house.

Or, if there are children around, take them outside for a **game** – they'll enjoy it and you won't feel as if exercise is a chore.

TOP TIP
Remember, the exercise needs to be **aerobic** – just enough to get you out of breath.

Create your exercise regime

First, look at your schedule and decide when you can fit in exercise – it needs to be **three** times a week for at least 30 minutes.

You don't have to do 30 minutes at first though – if you're unfit, start with just a few minutes at a time.

Always **warm up** properly before you exercise, and allow time for a **cool-down** routine at the end. The simplest way to do this is by starting and finishing slowly, for instance if you're jogging:

* Start walking gently.
* Speed up a little.
* Start to jog.
* Slow down to a fast walk.
* Walk gently.

You don't have to like it, you just have to do it!

If you've come to associate breathlessness with panic, then you might feel quite anxious about breathing hard during exercise. Don't push yourself over this, but gently **increase** the amount of exercise that you do, and the amount you let yourself get out of breath.

If you lack **motivation**, promise yourself a **treat** every time you hit your exercise target.

If you have physical or health restrictions, then talk to your doctor. **Swimming** is a beneficial exercise for many people, and there are clubs for people with physical disabilities.

Brain chemistry

Research has shown that regular exercise increases the levels of a chemical in the brain called **serotonin**. People suffering from panic often have low levels of this chemical. When serotonin levels are high, we feel more calm and cheerful and more in control, so it's well worth making sure that you have plenty of it.

Exercise also increases the **endorphins** in your brain. These also help you to feel more positive and less anxious.

Research into this topic is ongoing, and we still don't fully understand why exercise is so beneficial, but there's no doubt that it is.

Brain chemical increased by exercise	Possible effect
Serotonin	Calmer mood
Norepinephrine	Improved relaxation
Dopamine	Increased enjoyment
Endorphins	Positive mood

You can use exercise to increase your **relaxation response**.

To do this choose a repetitive exercise such as jogging, swimming or rowing. Avoid all distractions such as:

* exercising with a DVD
* listening to music through headphones.

Settle into a rhythm and allow your mind to be soothed by the rhythm of the physical actions.

It can help to repeat a simple **mantra** or **affirmation** in your mind in time to your rhythm.

Examples of mantras and affirmations:

* I can do this.
* I'm on the right path.
* It will be worth it.

34

CASE STUDY

Lesley loved games at school, but in her thirties she was too **busy** and **stressed** to think about sport. After her divorce she was even more stressed, and began to suffer from panic attacks.

She was advised to find more time for herself and find **enjoyable** activities, so she started going to the gym. She didn't enjoy it much, but realized that it was helping to reduce her panic so she kept going. Then one of her gym buddies decided to do a 10K run for charity. Lesley started to train alongside her, and from then on running was her exercise of choice.

CASE STUDY

Mike was horrified when his doctor told him that exercise could help with his panic attacks. He much preferred watching TV or online gaming. He already felt breathless most of the time, and was convinced that he'd keel over if he did exercise.

After a lot of persuasion he started to **walk** a little more, and then to **jog** – just from one lamp post to the next. He didn't enjoy this, but he coped with it and as a bonus he lost some weight.

On holiday he spent so much time in the pool that he realized he much preferred **swimming**, so now that is his exercise of choice.

4 Breathing

Retrain your breathing

You can take control and change your breathing

You are probably breathing **badly**, and you don't even realize it. Small children breathe naturally, but most adults in the Western world have lost the habit. We breathe from the top of the chest – too **shallow** and too **fast**. If you breathe like that, you're halfway to panic already.

It can be hard to change the bad habits of a lifetime, but you can learn to breathe slower and deeper.

* Most of us breathe too fast and too shallow.
* You should breathe from the **stomach**, not the chest.
* Breathing is automatic, but we have some control over it.
* Bad breathing upsets the balance of **gases** in your system.
* Practise breathing exercises regularly.
* **Emotions** affect breathing, and vice versa.

... slowing my breathing down, breathing in to a count of 6/8, breathing out to a count of 8.

Mal

About breathing

You can change your breathing and learn to breath **slowly**, **deeply** and **calmly**.

Shallow, fast breathing creates the ideal breeding ground for panic, so just by learning a different and healthier way of breathing you can make huge improvements to your **well-being**.

You can learn breathing exercises that you can use to change the way you breathe, working at your own pace, in small steps if that's what you need. It can take time to make changes, so don't rush.

Check your breathing

* Sit or lie *comfortably.*
* Place one hand on your *stomach* and one hand on your *chest*, at the top.
* What is each hand doing? Do they move as you breathe?

Many people find that the hand on their chest moves, but the hand on their stomach hardly moves at all. It should be the other way around!

Think about a small baby sleeping – watch one if you can. You'll see that the stomach moves in and out quite **naturally** as the baby breathes. If you have a pet cat or dog, watch it sleeping, and you'll see that the same is true of animals.

Hyperventilation

Breathing is controlled by your **autonomic nervous system**, which also looks after your internal organs and keeps you ticking over without your having to think about it. Luckily you are able to take some **control** of your breathing, which means that you can consciously correct any bad habits.

We breathe in oxygen and we breathe out carbon dioxide, but bad breathing upsets this balance and can be the cause of a lot of panicky feelings. You can gradually **retrain** your breathing, and you'll start to feel less panicky.

42

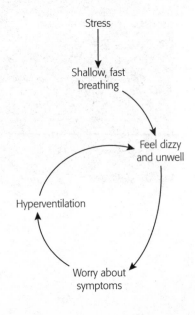

Stress

Shallow, fast breathing

Feel dizzy and unwell

Hyperventilation

Worry about symptoms

When you're **tense** and **anxious** your muscles tighten up and so does your breathing.

* Instead of slow, deep breaths, you take quick, shallow breaths.
* Instead of completely emptying your lungs of waste gases when you breathe out, you empty, perhaps, the top third, leaving the rest inside your lungs.

When the balance between oxygen and carbon dioxide is upset, you are likely to start feeling **light headed** and **disoriented.**

This is scary, and can make you even more anxious. It's purely physical, and, once you understand it, you can learn how to correct it.

Breathing exercises

Do breathing exercises for a few minutes several times a day. Start with this basic exercise.

1 Sit or lie *comfortably*.
2 Breathe *normally* for a few breaths.
3 Start to count as you breathe.
4 As you breathe in, count slowly to *four*.
5 As you breathe out, count slowly to *four*.

TOP TIP
If counting to four feels like too much for you, then count to two. If counting to four is pretty easy, then try counting to six or even eight.

Everyone has physical sensations, but most people take no notice of them.

Joanna, cognitive–behavioural therapist

Although we can take conscious control of our breathing, we rarely do, and our breathing changes all the time without our realising it. Some of the changes are physical – you breathe harder to run up stairs than you do to sit and watch TV. Some of the changes are emotional:

* Excitement can make you **breathless**.
* Distress can create **sobbing** breaths.
* Emotional pain can make you **hold** your breath.
* Sudden fright can make you **gasp**.

**Emotional breathing is a two-way street.
If you change your breathing,
you can change your emotions**

Breathing out gently

When you have a panic attack, all you want to do is suck **in** more and more breath. In fact, you need to breathe **out** long and slow, letting go of the panic.

1 Sit comfortably in front of a table.
2 Light a candle and set it in front of you.
  (Make sure that the candle is safe.)
3 Blow the candle out with one puff of breath.
4 Relight the candle.
5 Breathe out slowly and gently, just enough
  to make the candle flame flicker.
6 Do this for several breaths.

When you're comfortable with the basic breathing exercise, move on to this more advanced version.

1 Sit or lie *comfortably.*
2 Breathe *normally* for a few breaths.
3 Start to count as you breathe.
4 As you breathe in, count slowly to *four.*
5 As you breathe out, count slowly to *eight.*

By breathing out for a longer count than you breathe in, you will empty your lungs and restore the balance between oxygen and carbon dioxide in your system.

TOP TIP
Use this type of breathing for a few breaths whenever you're feeling stressed – it's very calming.

5 Meditation

Learn to meditate

Daily meditation is a highly effective stress buster

Practical meditation **reduces** stress and **combats** panic. It doesn't have to be religious or philosophical, and once you've learned how to do it you'll find it stands you in good stead for the rest of your life.

Meditation is not the same as relaxation. When you relax, both your mind and body let go and drift. When you meditate, your body is **still** but **poised**, and your mind is **alert**.

* Meditation is a great stress-busting tool.
* It helps you to **detach** from fearful thoughts.
* Meditate every day for 30–40 minutes.
* Simple meditation focuses on breathing or an object.
* A body scan puts you in touch with your body.
* Three-minute breathing space gives you a quick **calm-down**.
* Loving kindness meditation improves your **mood**.
* Meditation changes brain chemistry.

Meditation is like a window of calm in my day.

Lesley

About meditation

When you meditate you sit **quietly** on your own and focus **inwards**, ignoring external distractions. You also ignore your own mental chatter, letting your thoughts **drift** past you.

This will seem strange at first, but, if you repeat the practice daily, you'll gradually become **calmer** and less engaged with your fear-driven thoughts. You'll become more **detached** and able to observe yourself.

TOP TIP
Thoughts are like balloons floating in the blue sky of your mind. When you meditate, think of yourself as drifting quietly through the sky.

It was a great relief to know that ... I wasn't the only one who had had panic attacks.

Ann

To meditate you don't have to:

* wear funny clothes
* chant
* sit cross-legged
* join a religious group.

To meditate you do need to:

* be somewhere **quiet** and **private**
* turn off your phone
* sit **straight**, without leaning on a backrest
* allow enough **time** – about 30 minutes.

TOP TIP
If you find it hard to be alone with yourself, then have your choice of soothing quiet music playing while you meditate.

Aim to meditate every day. Start with a few minutes a day and build up to 30–40 minutes. **Early morning** is a good time, when the world is quiet.

Meditations

Meditation can help you **stabilize** your mood chemically, and the habit of observing your thoughts without engaging with them will help you **detach** yourself from panic.

Breathing meditation is the simplest form. All you do is sit still and breathe!

* Go somewhere quiet and private, turn off your phone, and sit comfortably with a straight back. Half-close your eyes and rest your gaze, unfocused, a few feet in front of you.
* Turn your attention to your **breathing**. Don't try to change it, just observe it. If it is shallow and panicky, then **accept** this. When you're ready, you'll breathe more slowly and calmly.
* If thoughts come into your mind, let them **drift** through. If you suddenly realize that you've become engaged with a thought, then let it go and return to the meditation.

54

Perhaps breathing meditation doesn't appeal to you, especially if you worry about your panicky breathing. If that's the case, you can meditate by focusing on an object, for instance:

1 a candle flame (make sure that the candle is safe)
2 a natural object, such as a shell, flower or piece of wood.

Set the object in front of you and let your gaze rest on it. If thoughts come into your mind, let them drift through, but don't engage with them. If you do find yourself thinking about something, gently bring your mind back to the meditation.

You can meditate by focusing on a candle flame or a natural object

Body scan and 3-minute breathing space

Body scan

1 Sit back or lie down.
2 Focus on your body.

Rather like relaxation, work around your **body**, but simply become **aware** of physical sensations.

Start with your left big toe, work up your leg, repeat with your right leg, torso, each arm and head and face.

Don't worry about your weight, fitness or any aches and pains. Just check the feelings of the moment and move on. When you reach places where you feel your panic, **breathe out** and let go of it.

Sometimes *emotions* are released during body scan. Take your time, allow yourself to feel them. Stop if you need to.

56

Use the 3-minute breathing space at intervals throughout the day

When things start to get too much, use this simple technique to **calm** and **ground** yourself. First, stop what you're doing, then follow the ABC:

* **Awareness** Check your body, giving it a quick body scan. Let go of your thoughts, and **accept** your emotions.
* **Breathing** Observe your breathing, don't try to change it. Feel the breath moving in and out. Focus on your stomach, which moves as you breathe.
* **Calmness** Let your awareness move out from your stomach into your whole body. Let **calmness** spread through your body.

It can be shorter than 3 minutes, but be sure to do all **three steps**.

Loving kindness meditation

After a few weeks of meditation you can try loving kindness, a more challenging meditation.

Spend a few minutes with your normal meditation. Once you're feeling **peaceful**, think about other people **kindly** and with **love** in the following order:

* yourself
* someone you love
* someone you know at a distance
* someone you dislike.

Practise this a few times, gradually extending your feelings of loving kindness out into the world. Then bring them back to your panicky thoughts and feelings. Panic is trying to **protect** you, so be **grateful**, but also accept that it's misguided and something you can **let go** of.

Meditation has a **powerful** effect on brain chemistry. People who meditate regularly show higher levels of the chemicals that induce feelings of **calm** and **well-being**, enhance sleep and reduce panic.

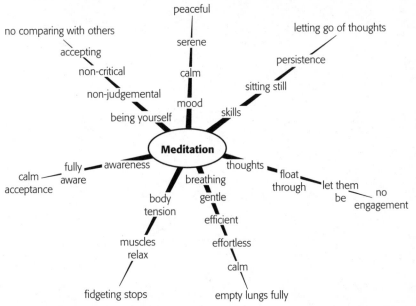

6 Food, drink and other substances

You are what you eat – and also what you drink and smoke

Everything you put into your body will have an effect on your well-being, so take the time to assess your needs

Your diet and eating habits can have a huge **impact** on your anxiety levels, both positive and negative.

If you eat and drink the right things, at the right time, you have a chance of **lowering** your anxiety and **reducing** the likelihood of a panic attack. If you make all the wrong decisions, you will **increase** anxiety and **raise** the likelihood of a panic attack.

* Re-assess everything you put into your body.
* Aim for a **stable** blood sugar level through a low GI (glycaemic index) diet.
* Drink plenty, but avoid caffeine and alcohol.
* Nicotine and other drugs provoke anxiety.
* Eat **regularly** through the day.
* Don't skip **breakfast**.

Certain additives in food and caffeine are stimulants which make me hyper.

Mal

Food and drink guidelines

A healthy diet with plenty of **fresh fruit and vegetables** is a good place to start. Carbohydrates with a **low GI** are good as they help keep your blood sugar level steady, and some also encourage serotonin production. The **B vitamins** are helpful for your nervous system, which needs repairing and replenishing following a panic attack and if you are constantly anxious.

Avoid foods with a high GI as they cause fluctuations in your **blood sugar**, which can create panicky feelings.

If you have a food sensitivity or intolerance, try to avoid that food, as it might contribute to your anxious feelings.

64

Dehydration can make you feel panicky. Drink water, fruit juice and milk to ensure that you stay **hydrated**.

Caffeine is **dehydrating**, and it also raises your heart rate and can make you feel very jittery. If you have a lot of caffeine, cut it down gradually. Sudden withdrawal can make you feel **unwell** for a day or two.

Alcohol **depresses** your nervous system (even if you think it cheers you up!). Try giving it up for a week or two and see if your anxiety improves. Never drink alcohol as a way of getting through a difficult situation – it will only make matters worse.

Organizing your diet

If your diet has a lot of elements that may be unhelpful in terms of your anxiety levels, change it slowly, one thing at a time.

Examples of helpful foods	Examples of foods to avoid
Wholemeal bread	White bread
Wholewheat pasta	Baked potatoes
Apples	Sweets
Lentils	Cakes
Chicken	Biscuits
Oats	Cornflakes
Brown rice	White rice
Bananas	Parsnips
Baked beans	Chips
Grapefruit	Watermelon
Eggs	Mashed potato
Fish	Alcohol
Nuts	Tea
Water	Coffee
Fruit juice	Cola
Milk	Energy drinks

66

Smokers usually feel that a cigarette relaxes them, but in fact nicotine has the opposite effect. If you smoke, then giving up will be the **best** thing you can do to help put a stop to panic attacks.

Some prescription drugs can create anxiety as a **side effect** – talk to your doctor about this. People withdrawing from **tranquillizers** can experience panic and anxiety – ask your doctor for help with this.

If you use street drugs, then it's time to **stop**. You can't be sure about side effects, and you may be making your anxiety and panic far worse. Try life without them for a while.

Fine tuning your diet

As well as what you eat, when you eat can make a big difference to how you feel.

Breakfast is the most important meal of the day. Eat something within **20 minutes** of waking up. It can be quite small, just to give your system some food (if you don't, and you start to rush about, you may start producing **adrenaline** to give you energy, and this will contribute to your anxiety).

Once you're properly awake, try to eat a more substantial **breakfast**. It doesn't have to be a full cooked breakfast, but choose something that will give you a good start to the day.

Eating little and often will help you stay calm by keeping your blood sugar steady

Dos

✔ Do eat something every **2 hours** or so. If you're worried about weight gain, make your main meals smaller.

✔ Do have a snack mid-morning, a light lunch, an afternoon snack, and dinner.

✔ Do eat something small (such as a banana) just before **bedtime**.

✔ Do eat **calmly** and take your time.

Don't

✘ Don't **skip** meals.

✘ Don't **bolt** down your food.

✘ Don't eat on the run between tasks.

Dealing with difficulties

* Anxiety can reduce your appetite and make you nauseous, but it's important to eat regularly if you want to feel **calmer**.
* Even one mouthful is better than not eating.
* Small portions look less daunting, so try eating **small amounts** throughout the day.
* Use lateral thinking: if you don't want a full meal, have a yoghurt, a smoothie or a piece of fruit.
* Many people can't face breakfast and eat later in the morning, but it's really important to **eat something first thing**.
* Even a sweet biscuit, which you should normally avoid, is better than nothing at breakfast time.

Make changes **slowly** – you will get there.

- ☐ Check with your doctor if you have health issues.
- ☐ Eat something soon after you **wake up**.
- ☐ Eat **breakfast** before you start your day.
- ☐ Eat every **2 hours**.
- ☐ Choose foods with a high GI.
- ☐ Avoid sweets and chocolates.
- ☐ Avoid cakes and biscuits.
- ☐ Avoid caffeine.
- ☐ Avoid alcohol.
- ☐ Give up or cut down on smoking.
- ☐ Give up non-prescribed drugs.
- ☐ Drink plenty of **water**.

7 Look after yourself

Take responsibility for caring for yourself

Caring for yourself is like being your own granny – ask yourself, what would she tell me to do?

Look at your life – are you **looking after yourself**? Everyone is busy nowadays, and it's easy to forget to include yourself in your schedule.

Mostly this is about **balance**. We all have to work – but not all the time. We have to look after the family, do chores, pay bills – but not all the time. We also need to have **fun** and **rest** both the mind and the body.

* Panic is often a warning that it's time to **slow down**.
* Check that you're looking after yourself properly.
* Check that you're not **overloaded** at work and at home.
* Make sure that you get enough good-quality **sleep**.
* Don't use sleep as an escape.
* Remember to have **fun**.

I am managing my levels of anxiety so they don't reach panic mode.

Mo

Time for self

For many people panic attacks are a **message** from their inner self. If you've ignored the little voice that's asking you to slow down, take a break and ease off a bit, then you don't leave it any option. Your inner self is determined to be heard so it hits you with the sledgehammer of a panic attack.

Now you have to **slow down**. But now you have panic to deal with as well. Luckily, it's not too late. If you start to look after yourself right now you will be able to deal with panic and get your life back in **balance**.

76

Ask yourself

* Am I **sleeping** well?
* Have I got enough time for **socializing**?
* Am I finding time for my **hobbies**?
* Am I coping well at **work**?
* Do I pay sufficient attention to my **relationships**?
* Do I find it easy to **delegate**?
* Do I spend time just **doing nothing**?

Look at any questions to which your answer is 'No' – they give you the clues as to where you're failing to care for yourself.

The 'No' answers also tell you where to make changes, so that you improve your quality of life.

Your commitments

There is no 'should' about it ...

It's easy to get bogged down in 'should' and 'ought to'. This is never helpful, and doubly so if you're struggling to deal with panic. Instead of **comparing yourself** with other people and **expecting too much** of yourself, start at the other end. Decide what you are capable of at this point in your life, how much you are able to give and what you need to take back for yourself.

Make a list of the things you **have** to do. Include:

1 paid work
2 work at home
3 your children
4 the rest of your family
5 voluntary work.

Your overall aim is to take the pressure off and free up more time for yourself

Now look through your list and decide if you are taking on **too much**. For each item on it, ask yourself:

* How **important** is this, really?
* If I **stopped** doing it, what would happen?
* Could **someone else** do it?

Look for things that you can give up, either permanently or temporarily, and things that you can ask other people to take on. You may be able to **rearrange** your schedule to make more efficient use of your time.

Sleep

If you're very **busy**, very **tense** and **worried** about your panic attacks, the chances are that you're not sleeping well. You may find it difficult to get off to sleep, or you may sleep fitfully, waking up throughout the night.

Look at your bedtime routine – do you **rush** around all evening and then scramble into bed with your mind **whirling**? Try half an hour of relaxing activity before bed. Establish a **wind-down routine** to ease yourself into sleep.

If you are still awake after 30 minutes, get up, go into another room and read or do a relaxation exercise. Then go back to bed and try again.

80

- ☐ Make your bedroom a **peaceful** place – no TVs or computers.
- ☐ Have a **comfortable** bed with a good mattress.
- ☐ Make sure the room is **warm** enough for you, and open the window every day to let fresh air in.
- ☐ Make the room as dark, or as light, as you like it to be.
- ☐ Eat a light supper, nothing heavy.
- ☐ No caffeine or alcohol in the 3 hours before bedtime.
- ☐ No daytime naps.

For some people sleep becomes an **escape** from anxiety and they sleep far too much. Try going to bed later and getting up earlier – your energy levels will adjust.

Remember to enjoy yourself

It's important to include time for **pleasure** – things that you do because you **enjoy** them. Whether you're shy or outgoing, social activities are very healthy. Building up your social network can give you a break from your own worries, help you get them back into perspective and also give you opportunities for support from friends.

Pleasurable activities can be anything from a big event (Christmas, a holiday), through smaller activities (a night out, regular club meetings), down to tiny things (a bubble bath, a takeaway, a phone call with an old friend).

Make time for all pleasureable activities, but especially the small things, as they require less input from you.

Worrying about panic, and recovering from panic attacks, can absorb a lot of **energy**. You can feel **overwhelmed** by having to manage panic as well as all your other chores and commitments. It's easy to forget to have **fun**, but putting the fun back into your life will be part of your recovery.

Fill in the chart below to show how you divide up your time now and how you'd like to divide it up – this will give you something to aim for.

	Percentage now	Percentage ideally
Work		
Hobbies/education		
Sleep		
Family/friends		
Chores		
Community		

8 Facing your fear

Face up to the fear of a panic attack

Fear is like a bully – it backs off when you challenge it

Panic attacks are **terrifying**, and the fear of having another one can become overwhelming. The panic lasts only a very short time, but the fear can be with you day and night. Experience has shown that **facing the fear** and learning to sit out the panic, if it comes, can be a very **effective** tool for recovery.

You can work out your own programme, or you can work with a therapist.

- ✷ Fear of having a panic attack can become **disabling**.
- ✷ A panic attack creates a surge of **energy**.
- ✷ Using the energy by moving away helps you feel better.
- ✷ Even if you stay put, the panic will **die down**.
- ✷ Facing fear in graduated steps is called exposure.
- ✷ Set **SMART** goals.
- ✷ Try some exposure **every day**.
- ✷ Keep going until you beat panic.

Facing your fear is a very, very hard thing to do. It's also the best – probably the only – way to learn that your most feared thing isn't that scary ... and that even if it did happen, you could cope.

Joanna, cognitive–behavioural therapist

The vicious circle of panic

A panic attack is an **extreme** reaction. The fight-or-flight response is short lived, designed to give you **energy** for action. When panic strikes, there is usually nothing to fight, so most people choose flight.

When you get up and leave, you start to feel better. This is because:

1 The panic was always going to be short lived.
2 You've used up some of the energy, which relieves some of the discomfort you feel.

But it can feel like the place was to **blame**, because you felt better when you left the place or situation. So you might decide never to go back there – in case you have another panic attack.

Panic will always come to a halt, whatever you do

For a while that can feel **good**, but perhaps you will have another panic attack, in another place or situation. Even if you don't, you may find yourself **avoiding** places and situations that remind you of the first one.

Pretty soon, you can find yourself with a **big problem** – everything you do and everywhere you go is **overshadowed** by the fear of having another panic attack.

This feels logical at the time, but it's all based on a **misunderstanding**. Your panic was always going to die down, even if you had stayed put. Hard to believe, but true.

Understanding exposure work

Exposure means learning to **face your fear**. It has two elements:

1 returning to places and situations you've been avoiding
2 learning that you can sit out a panic attack with no serious consequences.

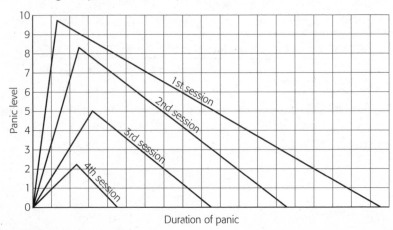

The graph shows that, as you repeat each step, your panic **reduces** in both intensity and time. (Note: you may need fewer or more sessions than shown.)

During exposure you face your fears in small **manageable** steps. You **repeat** each one until you feel comfortable with it – you may feel nervous at first, but during the repetition you will gradually learn to relax.

Look at the steps as a series of goals. It's easier to achieve goals if they're realistic in the first place. Make your goals SMART and **success** is more likely.

Specific	Not vague or generalized
Measurable	So you can be sure that you achieved it
Achievable	Within your ability
Relevant	Something you need to do
Time-bound	Achievable within a short time – 1 hour maximum

Planning exposure

Before you start, make sure that you have a good regime of **diet**, **exercise** and **relaxation**. Give it time to start working – 2 weeks at least. During that time you can make your plans.

Write down the details of your first panic attack – where you were, what you were doing and how you reacted.

Next, identify which aspects of the experience you are now **afraid** to face again.

Ask yourself

* What is it that I'm **avoiding**?
* How does this avoidance affect my life?
* How **important** is it for me to get over this?

Once you've **identified** your fears, decide how you'll **face** them. Break each one down into small manageable steps.

For instance, if your fear is busy supermarkets, start with a small shop at a quiet time and buy only one thing. You can choose how to move on – buy more things, go when it's busier, or go to a bigger shop – but change only one aspect at a time.

* Plan to do something **every day**.
* Start with the **easiest** fear for you.
* Start with the **smallest** step.
* Repeat each step until you feel **comfortable**.
* Only then move on to the **next step**.

Dealing with difficulties

Don't give up when you meet with difficulties – instead, look for **solutions**. Here are some common problems:

* **Impatience** There are no quick fixes and no miracle cures. Aim for **steady progress**. Keep a diary, so you can look back and see how far you've come.
* **Motivation** Sometimes you 'just won't feel like it.' Tell yourself you'll **do it anyway**.
* **Loneliness** Most people try to keep their problems to themselves, but it can help to **share your problems** with someone you trust. He or she may even be able to help you, but be careful not to become dependent.

* **Trying to do too much** Are your goals too big? Think of exposure as a **ladder** – the rungs need to be a reasonable distance apart, but not too far, or you won't be able to reach the next one.
* **Flat spots** If you run out of steam, coast for a while – **repeat** your recent goals so you don't slip back, and then move on to the next one.

Try these coping skills if you feel panicky:

* **Breathe** into a paper bag or cupped hands.
* **Distract** yourself mentally, with sums or by reciting song lyrics.
* Suck a mint.
* Listen to **soothing music** on your phone or MP3 player.

9 Negative thinking

Negative thinking feeds panic

Panic can become a habit, but habits can always be broken

Your first panic attack is usually caused by **stress**, but negative thinking can contribute to an ongoing panic problem.

You may **monitor** your body constantly, watching for the first signs of panic. You may develop a **fear of fear**, whereby you are frightened of having a panic attack. Or you may convince yourself that you will have a panic attack, and so, inevitably, you do.

- ❊ Negative thinking **fuels** panic.
- ❊ Decide if you're a worrier, a perfectionist, a critic or a victim.
- ❊ You may overgeneralize, tune out the good, ignore positives or lose your sense of proportion.
- ❊ You may expect the worst, catastrophize, be unrealistic or see only black or white.
- ❊ You may use emotional reasoning, jump to conclusions or dream.
- ❊ You may **blame** yourself or take things personally.

Panic comes from your thoughts. Slow down the intensity of the panic so you can work on the thoughts.

Mo

The four sub-personalities

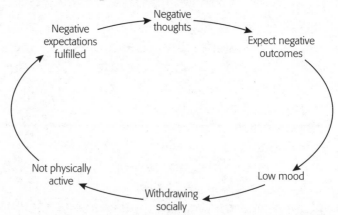

Negative thoughts

Negative expectations fulfilled

Expect negative outcomes

Not physically active

Low mood

Withdrawing socially

You can free yourself from negative thinking

Choose whichever of the following four sub-personalities is the **strongest** in you.

100

Bullet Guide: Beat Panic

WORRIERS constantly look for what could go wrong. They ask, 'What if…?', and always imagine that bad things will happen.

Solution Answer yourself, 'Perhaps the bad thing won't happen, and, anyway, I can't give in to worry.'

PERFECTIONISTS think that they'll never get it right and never be good enough. They say, 'I should …' or 'I ought to …'

Solution Tell yourself that you're only human, and no one is ever **perfect**. It's OK to be flawed.

CRITICS focus on what other people think of them. They **compare** themselves with others and always think that they're not as good as they are.

Solution Tell yourself that you can only be you, and that is **good enough**. You don't have to match up to other people.

VICTIMS feel that everything is out of their hands, and they don't have any say in what happens to them.

Solution Tell yourself that it's time to take **responsibility** – you can make changes. It does work.

Other types of negative thinking

Each one can be dealt with, once you've noticed it in yourself. If you have more than one, take them one at a time, starting with the one that feels **easiest**.

OVERGENERALIZING means **assuming** that you will have another panic attack when there is no real evidence that you will – just a feeling that you have.

Solution Tell yourself that you have no way of knowing what will happen.

TUNING OUT THE GOOD, you see only the bad things. You remember the last panic attack, but not the panic-free times since then.

Solution Keep a diary and record good times as well as bad.

IGNORING POSITIVES means that you can see good things, but you don't think that they **count**.

Solution Tell yourself that the good things all **matter** just as much as the bad.

NO SENSE OF PROPORTION means that you remember a panic attack as a tragedy, and barely recall times when you weren't panicky. You believe that you'll never recover.

Solution Focus on the good times, and accept that **recovery** happens in small steps.

More types of negative thinking

EXPECTING THE WORST means that you always expect bad outcomes. If you set a goal, you expect to **fail** at it.

Solution Tell yourself that it's better to try, even if you do fail, and, of course, you might **succeed**.

CATASTROPHIZING means that you don't just see bad outcomes, you see the **worst possible** outcomes. These thoughts are often vague.

Solution Tell yourself that no one knows what the **future** holds.

BEING UNREALISTIC means that small steps don't seem worth the bother, so you set recovery goals that are too ambitious, setting yourself up for **failure**.

Solution Try **smaller** steps, even if you can't see the point.

SEEING ONLY BLACK OR WHITE means that you notice only the **extremes**, and, if something isn't wholly wonderful, then you write it off as terrible.

Solution Treat yourself as if you were a frightened child, with **reassurance**, then remember that adults accept that the world has shades of grey in it.

> # People who experience panic attacks tend to choose the ... most catastrophic explanation for any sensation they don't like or understand.
>
> Joanna, cognitive–behavioural therapist

And more types of negative thinking

EMOTIONAL REASONING means that you rely on how you **feel** for decision making, even when feelings aren't appropriate.

Solution Check whether 'how I feel' is **relevant**.

JUMPING TO CONCLUSIONS means that you think you know why people behave as they do.

Solution Always look for **other explanations**. Understand that people often hide their feelings, or appear more confident than they really are.

DREAMING means that you think that other people do better than you. You **yearn** to be like them, but assume that it will never happen.

Solution Tell yourself that **you are you**, which is a good start, and that you can always **choose** to make changes.

FEELING TO BLAME means that you feel **responsible** for making people around you happy and safe.

Solution Tell yourself that it's better to respect the **right** of other people to shape their own lives.

TAKING THINGS PERSONALLY means that you think that everything is aimed at you.

If someone ignores you, you **assume** that they were deliberately snubbing you, not that they just didn't see you.

Solution Always look for **other explanations**.

CALLING YOURSELF NAMES means that you use words such as 'lazy', 'useless' and 'pathetic' about yourself.

Solution Ask yourself where you got these words from – usually it goes back to childhood. Then **ban** yourself from using them.

10 Why me?

Sometimes it seems that life isn't fair

Panic strikes when you least expect it, usually when you think the worst is over

The fight-or-flight mechanism is there to help us cope with immediate danger. We use it to get through all sorts of **stress**, whether it's short and sharp or ongoing. Quite often panic strikes just at the point when the **pressure** is off, just when you thought you'd be able to take a break.

Somehow you've **ignored** your own needs for too long and you're stuck in fight-or-flight mode.

* Panic often starts after a **stressful** period.
* You can **assess** your stress.
* Stress can be a sudden crisis or long term.
* Chronic panic can be due to **suppressed emotions**.
* You can learn to release your emotions safely.
* You may need to make **big changes**.
* **Help** is available.

You must understand what creates stress for you and how you habitually respond to it; then learn that there are other ways of responding and be prepared to try a step-by-step approach.

Emma

Stress builds up over time, and we all have our tipping point

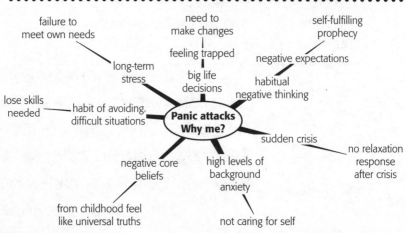

failure to meet own needs

need to make changes

self-fulfilling prophecy

long-term stress

feeling trapped

negative expectations

big life decisions

habitual negative thinking

lose skills needed

habit of avoiding difficult situations

Panic attacks Why me?

sudden crisis

no relaxation response after crisis

negative core beliefs

high levels of background anxiety

from childhood feel like universal truths

not caring for self

No one can keep going **forever**. Panic attacks are only one possible response – for instance, some people develop depression, and some break down entirely.

Think about your life over the **2 years** before your first panic attack. Look at the **stress factors** and accept that they must have contributed to your first attack. Anything from divorce to a difficult time at Christmas will add to your stress, as well as ongoing problems such as overwork.

Ask yourself

* Is my **breathing** shallow and rapid?
* Do I do **too much**?
* Am I **irritable**?
* Do I feel that **nobody cares**?
* Do I feel hard done by?
* Do I feel **overwhelmed**?
* Am I always right?
* Do I have to **rush** to get everything done?
* Do I sweat a lot?
* Do I have a dry mouth?
* Do I get shaky?
* Does it all seem **pointless**?
* Am I always the one who does everything?

The more questions you answer 'Yes' to, the more stressed you are.

Types of stress

Some stress is caused by a **sudden crisis** – someone is ill, or bad news arrives. The fight-or-flight mechanism cuts in and you **get through**, perhaps with little sleep, skipping meals and constant worry.

When the crisis is over, you feel relieved. You just want to get back to **normal** as quickly as possible. There's probably a lot to catch up on, if you had to let things slide at home and work, so perhaps you throw yourself into it.

Panic attacks can start if you forget to allow enough time to get over the crisis. You need to **replenish** the mental and physical resources you used to get through it.

114

Some stress is the result of a **gradual** build-up. As time goes by and you take on more and more, you can easily forget to leave **down time** in your schedule.

Whether it's overload at work, looking after children or caring for family members who are old or ill, you can end up convinced that you have to make everything OK for everybody else.

Someone doing this is also using up **resources** without replenishing them. Sooner or later, something's got to give – that's when the panic attacks start.

For these people panic is a **message** from deep inside them, telling them that they need to look after their own needs.

Stress and emotions

For some people panic becomes **chronic** and they live with it for years. This can be because they fail to take care of themselves properly, but also it may be that **repressed emotions** are feeding the panic.

Despair, **anger** and **grief** are strong emotions that can be difficult to express, and yet can be very damaging if they're held inside.

It can help to learn to communicate assertively. This means speaking up for yourself without becoming either aggressive or defensive. If you find that difficult, look for a class near you or read a book about assertiveness.

Learning to express withheld feelings can be an important part of recovery from panic. You can:

* **Talk** to someone you feel safe with.
* **Write** it all out – you can always destroy the writing afterwards if it contains secrets.
* **Unblock** your feelings with music or an emotional film.
* **Thump** a cushion, **yell**, **shout** or play sport.

Allow **time** for releasing your emotions, and take it in small steps so that you don't feel overwhelmed.

Looking at change

As you think through your experience of panic, and your individual situation, you may begin to realize that **big life changes** are needed. This can be difficult to accept if you've **invested** a lot in the way you live now, or if you feel too **exhausted** to make important decisions.

Don't rush it. Allow yourself time to think things through. You may need to look at:

* your job
* your family life
* your partner.

Changing jobs may mean retraining, or less money. Changing family dynamics can lead to you feeling guilty. And leaving a partner is one of the biggest decisions any of us will ever make.

You don't have to be alone with your problems. Ask your doctor for help with panic attacks. The accepted therapy is called **cognitive–behavioural therapy**, also known as CBT, so ask for a referral. CBT looks at both your thoughts and your actions and teaches you ways of modifying both.

For dealing with repressed emotions and looking back into the past, consider seeing a **counsellor.**

For help with all types of relationships, talk to someone at **Relate**.

Further reading

The Anxiety and Phobia Workbook by Edmund J. Bourne (New Harbinger Publications, 2011).

Essential Help for your Nerves by Claire Weekes (Thorsons, 2000).

Feel the Fear and Do It Anyway: How to Turn Your Fear and Indecision into Confidence and Action by Susan Jeffers (Vermilion, 2007).

Free Yourself from Anxiety: A Self-help Guide to Overcoming Anxiety Disorders by Emma Fletcher and Martha Langley (How To Books, 2009).

Organizations

No Panic: www.nopanic.org.uk; helpline 0808 808 0545.